On Loving God by St. Bernard de Clairvaux
ISBN 978-1-387-91730-3
Copyright ©2018 by Peter G. Epps

ON LOVING GOD

by
St. Bernard de Clairvaux (A.D. 1090-1153)

edited by Peter G. Epps

Contents

On Loving God
St. Bernard of Clairvaux

Dedication

T O THE ILLUSTRIOUS Lord Haimeric, Cardinal Deacon of the Roman Church, and Chancellor: Bernard, called Abbot of Clairvaux, wisheth long life in the Lord and death in the Lord.

Hitherto you have been wont to seek prayers from me, not the solving of problems; although I count myself sufficient for neither. My profession shows that, if not my conversation; and to speak truth, I lack the diligence and the ability that are most essential. Yet I am glad that you turn again for spiritual counsel, instead of busying yourself about carnal matters: I only wish you had gone to some one better equipped than I am. Still, learned and simple give the same excuse and one can hardly tell whether it comes from modesty or from ignorance, unless obedience to the task assigned shall reveal. So, take from my poverty what I can give you, lest I should seem to play the philosopher, by reason of my silence.

Only, I do not promise to answer other questions you may raise. This one, as to loving God, I will deal with as He shall teach me; for it is sweetest, it can be handled most safely, and it will be most profitable. Keep the others for wiser men.

Expression of humility and deference, here, but notice also the hint of sarcasm, indicating writer and reader are on friendly terms.

Chapter I. Why we should love God

YOU WANT ME to tell you why God is to be loved and how much. I answer, the reason for loving God is God Himself; and the measure of love due to Him is immeasurable love. Is this plain? Doubtless, to a thoughtful man; but I am debtor to the unwise also. *Again the mix of humor and humility, here.* A word to the wise is sufficient; but I must consider simple folk too. Therefore I set myself joyfully to explain more in detail what is meant above.

We are to love God for Himself, because of a twofold reason; nothing is more reasonable, nothing more profitable. When one asks, Why should I love God? he may mean, What is lovely in God? or What shall I gain by loving God? In either case, the same sufficient cause of love exists, namely, God Himself.

And first, of His title to our love. Could any title be greater than this, that He gave Himself for us unworthy wretches? And being God, what better gift could He offer than Himself? Hence, if one seeks for God's claim upon our love here is the chiefest: Because He first loved us. *I John 4.19*

Ought He not to be loved in return, when we think who loved, whom He loved, and how much He loved? For who is He that loved? The same of whom every spirit testifies: *Ps. 16:2, Vulg.* Thou art my God: my goods are nothing unto Thee. And is not His love that wonderful charity which seeketh not her *1 Cor 13:5* own? But for whom was such unutterable love made manifest? The apostle tells us: When we were enemies, we were *Rom. 5:10* reconciled to God by the death of His Son. So it was God who loved us, loved us freely, and loved us while yet we were enemies. And how great was this love of His? St. John answers: God so loved the world that He gave His only-*John 3.16* begotten Son, that whosoever believeth in Him should not *Rom. 8:32* perish, but have everlasting life. St. Paul adds: He spared not His own Son, but delivered Him up for us all; and the Son *John 15.13* says of Himself, Greater love hath no man than this, that a man lay down his life for his friends.

This is the claim which God the holy, the supreme, the omnipotent, has upon men, defiled and base and weak. Some one may urge that this is true of mankind, but not of angels. True, since for angels it was not needful. He who succored men in their time of need, preserved angels from such need; and even as His love for sinful men wrought wondrously in them so that they should not remain sinful, so that same love which in equal measure He poured out upon angels kept them altogether free from sin.

Chapter II. How much God deserves love

THOSE WHO ADMIT the truth of what I have said know, I am sure, why we are bound to love God. But if unbelievers will not grant it, their ingratitude is at once confounded by His innumerable benefits, lavished on our race, and plainly discerned by the senses. Who is it that gives food to all flesh, light to every eye, air to all that breathe? It would be foolish to begin a catalogue, since I have just called them innumerable: but I name, as notable instances, food, sunlight and air; not because they are God's best gifts, but because they are essential to bodily life. Man must seek in his own higher nature for the highest gifts; and these are dignity, wisdom and virtue. By dignity I mean *Dignity* free-will, whereby he not only excels all other earthly creatures, but has dominion over them.   Wisdom is the power *Wisdom* whereby he recognizes this dignity, and perceives also that it is no accomplishment of his own. And virtue impels man *Virtue* to seek eagerly for Him who is man's Source, and to lay fast hold on Him when He has been found.

Now, these three best gifts have each a twofold character. *Analogical* Dignity appears not only as the prerogative of human nature, *development,* but also as the cause of that fear and dread of man which is *here: Each* upon every beast of the earth. Wisdom perceives this distinc- *term has a* tion, but owns that though in us, it is, like all good qualities, *paradoxical* not of us. And lastly, virtue moves us to search eagerly for *limit that* an Author, and, when we have found Him, teaches us to *indicates the next.*

cling to Him yet more eagerly. Consider too that dignity
without wisdom is nothing worth; and wisdom is harmful
without virtue, as this argument following shows: There is
no glory in having a gift without knowing it. But to know
only that you have it, without knowing that it is not of
yourself that you have it, means self-glorying, but no true
glory in God. And so the apostle says to men in such cases,
What hast thou that thou didst not receive? Now, if thou
didst receive it, why dost thou glory as if thou hadst not
received it? He asks, Why dost thou glory? but goes on, as
if thou hadst not received it, showing that the guilt is not in
glorying over a possession, but in glorying as though it had
not been received. And rightly such glorying is called vain-
glory, since it has not the solid foundation of truth. The
apostle shows how to discern the true glory from the false,
when he says, He that glorieth, let him glory in the Lord,
that is, in the Truth, since our Lord is Truth.

We must know, then, what we are, and that it is not of
ourselves that we are what we are. Unless we know this
thoroughly, either we shall not glory at all, or our glorying
will be vain. Finally, it is written, If thou know not, go thy
way forth by the footsteps of the flock. And this is right. For
man, being in honor, if he know not his own honor, may
fitly be compared, because of such ignorance, to the beasts
that perish. Not knowing himself as the creature that is
distinguished from the irrational brutes by the possession
of reason, he commences to be confounded with them

Quotable

1 Cor. 4:7

1 Cor 1:31
John 14:6

Good to exult
in creaturely
goodness!
Cant. 1:8

because, ignorant of his own true glory which is within, he is led captive by his curiosity, and concerns himself with external, sensual things. So he is made to resemble the lower orders by not knowing that he has been more highly endowed than they.

We must be on our guard against this ignorance. We must *Human* not rank ourselves too low; and with still greater care we *dignity is* must see that we do not think of ourselves more highly than *defaced* we ought to think, as happens when we foolishly impute to *lacks basic* ourselves whatever good may be in us. But far more than *education.* either of these kinds of ignorance, we must hate and shun that presumption which would lead us to glory in goods not *Presump-* our own, knowing that they are not of ourselves but of God, *tion is still* and yet not fearing to rob God of the honor due unto Him. *worse,* For mere ignorance, as in the first instance, does not glory *though.* at all; and mere wisdom, as in the second, while it has a kind of glory, yet does not glory in the Lord. In the third evil case, however, man sins not in ignorance but deliberately, usurping the glory which belongs to God. And this arrogance is a *Arrogance* more grievous and deadly fault than the ignorance of the *is the* second, since it contemns God, while the other knows Him *worst.* not. Ignorance is brutal, arrogance is devilish. Pride only, the chief of all iniquities, can make us treat gifts as if they were rightful attributes of our nature, and, while receiving benefits, rob our Benefactor of His due glory.

Wherefore to dignity and wisdom we must add virtue, the proper fruit of them both. Virtue seeks and finds Him who is the Author and Giver of all good, and who must be in all things glorified; otherwise, one who knows what is right yet *Luke 12:47* fails to perform it, will be beaten with many stripes. Why? you may ask. Because he has failed to put his knowledge to *Ps. 36:4* good effect, but rather has imagined mischief upon his bed; like a wicked servant, he has turned aside to seize the glory *Refers to* which, his own knowledge assured him, belonged only to *the famil-* his good Lord and Master. It is plain, therefore, that dignity *iar incipit-* *Non nobis,* without wisdom is useless and that wisdom without virtue *Domine,* is accursed. But when one possesses virtue, then wisdom and *non nobis,* dignity are not dangerous but blessed. Such a man calls on *sed nomini* God and lauds Him, confessing from a full heart, Not unto *tuo da glo-* us, O Lord, not unto us, but unto Thy name give glory. *riam.* *Ps. 113:1* Which is to say, O Lord, we claim no knowledge, no distinction for ourselves; all is Thine, since from Thee all things do come.

But we have digressed too far in the wish to prove that even those who know not Christ are sufficiently admonished by the natural law, and by their own endowments of soul and body, to love God for God's own sake. To sum up: what infidel does not know that he has received light, air, food— all things necessary for his own body's life—from Him alone *Ps. 136:25* who giveth food to all flesh, who maketh His sun to rise on *Matt. 5:45* the evil and on the good, and sendeth rain on the just and on the unjust. Who is so impious as to attribute the peculiar eminence of humanity to any other except to Him who saith, in Genesis, Let us make man in Our image, after Our

likeness'? Who else could be the Bestower of wisdom, but *Gen. 1:26*
He that teacheth man knowledge? Who else could bestow *Ps. 94:10*
virtue except the Lord of virtue? Therefore even the infidel
who knows not Christ but does at least know himself, is
bound to love God for God's own sake. He is unpardonable
if he does not love the Lord his God with all his heart, and
with all his soul, and with all his mind; for his own innate
justice and common sense cry out from within that he is
bound wholly to love God, from whom he has received all
things. But it is hard, nay rather, impossible, for a man by
his own strength or in the power of free-will to render all
things to God from whom they came, without rather
turning them aside, each to his own account, even as it is
written, For all seek their own; and again, The imagination *Phil. 2:21*
of man's heart is evil from his youth.   *Gen. 8:21*

VIRTUE
impels man
to seek eagerly
for him who is man's
SOURCE,
& to lay fast hold
on him when he has been
FOUND.

Chapter III. The incentives Christians have to love God

THE FAITHFUL KNOW how much need they have of Jesus and Him crucified; but though they wonder and rejoice at the ineffable love made manifest in Him, they are not daunted at having no more than their own poor souls to give in return for such great and condescending charity. They love all the more, because they know themselves to be loved so exceedingly; but to whom little is given the same loveth little. Neither Jew nor *Luke 7:47* pagan feels the pangs of love as doth the Church, which saith, Stay me with flagons, comfort me with apples; for I am sick of love. She beholds King Solomon, with the crown where-*Cant. 2:5* with his mother crowned him in the day of his espousals; she sees the Sole-begotten of the Father bearing the heavy *Reading* burden of His Cross; she sees the Lord of all power and *Song of* might bruised and spat upon, the Author of life and glory *Solomon* transfixed with nails, smitten by the lance, overwhelmed *(Canticle) as* with mockery, and at last laying down His precious life for *Christ's* His friends. Contemplating this the sword of love pierces *love for* through her own soul also and she cried aloud, Stay me with *His Church,* flagons, comfort me with apples; for I am sick of love. The *and hers for* fruits which the Spouse gathers from the Tree of Life in the *Him.* midst of the garden of her Beloved, are pomegranates, *Cant. 4:13* borrowing their taste from the Bread of heaven, and their color from the Blood of Christ. She sees death dying and its author overthrown: she beholds captivity led captive from hell to earth, from earth to heaven, so that at the name of Jesus every knee should bow, of things in heaven and things *Phil. 2:10* in earth and things under the earth. The earth under the ancient curse brought forth thorns and thistles; but now the Church beholds it laughing with flowers and restored by the grace of a new benediction. Mindful of the verse, My heart danceth for joy, and in my song will I praise Him, she refreshes herself with the fruits of His Passion which she gathers from the Tree of the Cross, and with the flowers of His Resurrection whose fragrance invites the frequent visits of her Spouse.

Then it is that He exclaims, Behold thou art fair, My *Cant. 1:16* beloved, yea pleasant: also our bed is green. She shows her desire for His coming and whence she hopes to obtain it; not because of her own merits but because of the flowers of *Christ being* that field which God hath blessed. Christ who willed to be *eternal God* conceived and brought up in Nazareth, that is, the town of *uniquely* branches, delights in such blossoms. Pleased by such heav- *chose His* enly fragrance the bridegroom rejoices to revisit the heart's *own human* chamber when He finds it adorned with fruits and decked *Mother and* with flowers—that is, meditating on the mystery of His *birthplace!* Passion or on the glory of His Resurrection.

The tokens of the Passion we recognize as the fruitage of the ages of the past, appearing in the fullness of time during *Gal. 4:4* the reign of sin and death. But it is the glory of the Resurrection, in the new springtime of regenerating grace, that the fresh flowers of the later age come forth, whose fruit shall be given without measure at the general resurrection, when time shall be no more. And so it is written, The winter is past, the rain is over and gone, the flowers appear on the earth; signifying that summer has come back with Him who *Cant. 2:11 ff* dissolves icy death into the spring of a new life and says, Behold, I make all things new. His Body sown in the grave *Rev. 21:5* has blossomed in the Resurrection; and in like manner our *1 Cor. 15:42* valleys and fields which were barren or frozen, as if dead, glow with reviving life and warmth.

The Father of Christ who makes all things new, is well pleased with the freshness of those flowers and fruits, and the beauty of the field which breathes forth such heavenly fragrance; and He says in benediction, See, the smell of My Son is as the smell of a field which the Lord hath blessed. *Gen. 27:17* Blessed to overflowing, indeed, since of His fullness have all *John 1:16* we received. But the Bride may come when she pleases and *The* gather flowers and fruits therewith to adorn the inmost *Church has* recesses of her conscience; that the Bridegroom when He *every right* cometh may find the chamber of her heart redolent with *to all Christ* perfume. *has given* *her.*

So it behoves us, if we would have Christ for a frequent guest, to fill our hearts with faithful meditations on the mercy He showed in dying for us, and on His mighty power in rising again from the dead. To this David testified when he sang, God spake once, and twice I have also heard the same; that power belongeth unto God; and that Thou, Lord, art merciful. And surely there is proof enough and to spare *Ps 62:11 ff* in that Christ died for our sins and rose again for our justification, and ascended into heaven that He might protect us from on high, and sent the Holy Spirit for our comfort. Hereafter He will come again for the consummation of our bliss. In His Death He displayed His mercy, in His Resurrection His power; both combine to manifest His glory.

The Bride desires to be stayed with flagons and comforted with apples, because she knows how easily the warmth of love can languish and grow cold; but such helps are only until she has entered into the bride chamber. There she will receive His long-desired caresses even as she sighs, His left hand is under my head and His right hand doth embrace me. *Cant. 2:6* Then she will perceive how far the embrace of the right hand excels all sweetness, and that the left hand with which He at first caressed her cannot be compared to it. She will understand what she has heard: It is the spirit that quickeneth; the *John 6:63* flesh profiteth nothing. She will prove what she hath read: My memorial is sweeter than honey, and mine inheritance *Ecclus. 24:20* than the honey-comb. What is written elsewhere, The *Ps. 145:7* memorial of Thine abundant kindness shall be showed, refers doubtless to those of whom the Psalmist had said just before: One generation shall praise Thy works unto another *Ps. 145:4* and declare Thy power. Among us on the earth there is His memory; but in the Kingdom of heaven His very Presence. That Presence is the joy of those who have already attained to beatitude; the memory is the comfort of us who are still wayfarers, journeying towards the Fatherland.

Chapter IV. Of those who find comfort in God

B UT IT WILL be well to note what class of people takes comfort in the thought of God. Surely not that perverse and crooked generation to whom it was said, Woe unto you that are rich; for ye have received your consolation. Rather, those who can say with truth, My soul *Luke 6:24* refuseth comfort. For it is meet that those who are not *Ps. 77:2* satisfied by the present should be sustained by the thought of the future, and that the contemplation of eternal happiness should solace those who scorn to drink from the river of transitory joys. That is the generation of them that seek the Lord, even of them that seek, not their own, but the face of the God of Jacob. To them that long for the presence of the living God, the thought of Him is sweetest itself: but there is no satiety, rather an ever-increasing appetite, even as the Scripture bears witness, they that eat me shall yet be hungry; and if the one an-hungred spake, When I awake up *Ecclus. 24:21* after Thy likeness, I shall be satisfied with it. Yea, blessed even now are they which do hunger and thirst after righteousness, for they, and they only, shall be filled. Woe to you, wicked and perverse generation; woe to you, foolish and abandoned people, who hate Christ's memory, and dread His second Advent!

Well may you fear, who will not now seek deliverance from the snare of the hunter; because they that will be rich fall into temptation and a snare, and into many foolish and

1 Tim. 6:9 hurtful lusts. In that day we shall not escape the dreadful sentence of condemnation, Depart from Me, ye cursed, into *Matt. 25:41* everlasting fire. O dreadful sentence indeed, O hard saying! How much harder to bear than that other saying which we repeat daily in church, in memory of the Passion: Whoso eateth My flesh and drinketh My blood hath eternal life. *John 6:54* That signifies, whoso honors My death and after My *Col. 3:5* example mortifies his members which are upon the earth shall have eternal life, even as the apostle says, If we suffer, *2 Tim. 2:12* we shall also reign with Him. And yet many even today recoil from these words and go away, saying by their action if not *John 6:60* with their lips, This is a hard saying; who can hear it? A generation that set not their heart aright, and whose spirit *Ps. 78:8* cleaveth not steadfastly unto God, but chooseth rather to trust in uncertain riches, it is disturbed at the very name of the Cross, and counts the memory of the Passion intolerable. How can such sustain the burden of that fearful sentence, Depart from Me, ye cursed, into everlasting fire, prepared for the devil and his angels?   On whomsoever that stone *Luke 20:18* shall fall it will grind him to powder; but the generation of *Ps. 112:2* the faithful shall be blessed, since, like the apostle, they labor that whether present or absent they may be accepted of the *2 Cor. 5:9* Lord. At the last day they too shall hear the Judge pronounce their award, Come, ye blessed of My Father, inherit the *Matt. 25:34* kingdom prepared for you from the foundation of the world.

In that day those who set not their hearts aright will feel, too late, how easy is Christ's yoke, to which they would not bend their necks and how light His burden, in comparison with the pains they must then endure. O wretched slaves of Mammon, you cannot glory in the Cross of our Lord Jesus Christ while you trust in treasures laid up on earth: you cannot taste and see how gracious the Lord is, while you are hungering for gold. If you have not rejoiced at the thought of His coming, that day will be indeed a day of wrath to you. *"You cannot serve both God and Mammon" Matt. 6:24*

But the believing soul longs and faints for God; she rests sweetly in the contemplation of Him. She glories in the reproach of the Cross, until the glory of His face shall be revealed. Like the Bride, the dove of Christ, that is covered with silver wings, white with innocence and purity, she reposes in the thought of Thine abundant kindness, Lord Jesus; and above all she longs for that day when in the joyful splendor of Thy saints, gleaming with the radiance of the Beatific Vision, her feathers shall be like gold, resplendent with the joy of Thy countenance. *Ps. 68:13*

Rightly then may she exult, His left hand is under my head and His right hand doth embrace me. The left hand signifies the memory of that matchless love, which moved Him to lay down His life for His friends; and the right hand is the Beatific Vision which He hath promised to His own, and the delight they have in His presence. The Psalmist sings rapturously, At Thy right hand there is pleasure for evermore: so we are warranted in explaining the right hand as that divine and deifying joy of His presence. *Ps. 16:11 "Deifying" cf. 2 Pet. 1:3-4*

Rightly too is that wondrous and ever-memorable love symbolized as His left hand, upon which the Bride rests her head until iniquity be done away: for He sustains the purpose of her mind, lest it should be turned aside to earthly, carnal desires. For the flesh wars against the spirit: The corruptible body presseth down the soul, and the earthly tabernacle weigheth down the mind that museth upon many *Wisdom 9:15* things. What could result from the contemplation of compassion so marvelous and so undeserved, favor so free and so well attested, kindness so unexpected, clemency so unconquerable, grace so amazing except that the soul should withdraw from all sinful affections, reject all that is inconsistent with God's love, and yield herself wholly to heavenly things? No wonder is it that the Bride, moved by the perfume of these unctions, runs swiftly, all on fire with love, yet reckons herself as loving all too little in return for the Bridegroom's love. And rightly, since it is no great matter that a little dust should be all consumed with love of that Majesty which loved her first and which revealed itself as wholly bent on saving her. For God so loved the world that He gave His only-begotten Son, that whosoever believeth *John 3:16* in Him should not perish but have everlasting life. This sets forth the Father's love. But He hath poured out His soul *Isa. 53:12* unto death, was written of the Son. And of the Holy Spirit it is said, The Comforter which is the Holy Ghost whom the Father will send in My name, He shall teach you all things, and bring all things to your remembrance, whatsoever I have said unto you. It is plain, therefore, that God loves us, and *John 14:26* loves us with all His heart; for the Holy Trinity altogether loves us, if we may venture so to speak of the infinite and incomprehensible Godhead who is essentially one.

She glories in the
reproach of the
CROSS,
until the
GLORY
of his face
shall be
REVEALED.

Chapter V. The Christian's debt of love

FROM THE CONTEMPLATION of what has been
said, we see plainly that God is to be loved, and that *An "infidel"*
He has a just claim upon our love. But the infidel *is someone who has not*
does not acknowledge the Son of God, and so he can know *received*
neither the Father nor the Holy Spirit; for he that honoureth *the faith.*
not the Son, honoureth not the Father which sent Him, nor
the Spirit whom He hath sent. He knows less of God than *John 5:23*
we; no wonder that he loves God less. This much he under-
stands at least—that he owes all he is to his Creator. But how
will it be with me? For I know that my God is not merely
the bounteous Bestower of my life, the generous Provider
for all my needs, the pitiful Consoler of all my sorrows, the
wise Guide of my course: but that He is far more than all
that. He saves me with an abundant deliverance: He is my
eternal Preserver, the portion of my inheritance, my glory.
Even so it is written, With Him is plenteous redemption;
and again, He entered in once into the holy place, having *Ps. 130:7*
obtained eternal redemption for us. Of His salvation it is *Heb. 9:12*
written, He forsaketh not His that be godly; but they are
preserved for ever; and of His bounty, Good measure, *Ps. 37:28*
pressed down and shaken together, and running over, shall
men give into your bosom; and in another place, Eye hath *Luke 6:38*
not seen nor ear heard, neither have entered into the heart
of man, those things which God hath prepared for them that
love Him. He will glorify us, even as the apostle beareth *1 Cor. 2:9*

witness, saying, We look for the Savior, the Lord Jesus Christ, who shall change our vile body that it may be fashioned like *Phil. 3:20 ff* unto His glorious body; and again, I reckon that the sufferings of this present time are not worthy to be compared with *Rom. 8:18* the glory which shall be revealed in us; and once more, Our light affliction, which is but for a moment, worketh for us a far more exceeding and eternal weight of glory; while we look not at the things which are seen, but at the things which *2 Cor. 4:17ff* are not seen.

' What shall I render unto the Lord for all His benefits *Ps. 116:12* towards me?. Reason and natural justice alike move me to give up myself wholly to loving Him to whom I owe all that *Progression* I have and am. But faith shows me that I should love Him *from* far more than I love myself, as I come to realize that He hath *nature by* given me not my own life only, but even Himself. Yet, before *faith to* *charity with* the time of full revelation had come, before the Word was *God.* made flesh, died on the Cross, came forth from the grave, and returned to His Father; before God had shown us how much He loved us by all this plenitude of grace, the commandment had been uttered, Thou shalt love the Lord thy God with all thine heart, and with all thy soul and with all *Deut. 6:5* thy might, that is, with all thy being, all thy knowledge, all thy powers. And it was not unjust for God to claim this from His own work and gifts. Why should not the creature love his Creator, who gave him the power to love? Why should he not love Him with all his being, since it is by His gift alone that he can do anything that is good? It was God's creative grace that out of nothingness raised us to the dignity of manhood; and from this appears our duty to love Him, and the justice of His claim to that love. But how infinitely is the benefit increased when we bethink ourselves of His fulfillment of the promise, thou, Lord, shalt save both man and beast: how excellent is Thy mercy, O Lord! For we, who *Ps. 36:6 ff* turned our glory into the similitude of a calf that eateth hay, *Ps. 106:20* by our evil deeds debased ourselves so that we might be compared unto the beasts that perish. I owe all that I am to Him who made me: but how can I pay my debt to Him who redeemed me, and in such wondrous wise? Creation was not so vast a work as redemption; for it is written of man and of all things that were made, He spake the word, and they were made. But to redeem that creation which sprang into being *Ps. 148:5* at His word, how much He spake, what wonders He wrought, what hardships He endured, what shames He suffered! Therefore what reward shall I give unto the Lord for all the benefits which He hath done unto me? In the first creation He gave me myself; but in His new creation He gave me Himself, and by that gift restored to me the self that I had lost. Created first and then restored, I owe Him myself twice over in return for myself. But what have I to offer Him for the gift of Himself? Could I multiply myself a thousand-fold and then give Him all, what would that be in comparison with God?

In the first
CREATION
he gave me
MYSELF;

but in his new
CREATION
he gave me
HIMSELF.

Chapter VI. A brief summary

ADMIT THAT GOD deserves to be loved very much, yea, boundlessly, because He loved us first, He infinite and we nothing, loved us, miserable sinners, with a love so great and so free. This is why I said at the beginning that the measure of our love to God is to love immeasurably. For since our love is toward God, who is infinite and immeasurable, how can we bound or limit the love we owe Him? Besides, our love is not a gift but a debt. And since it is the Godhead who loves us, Himself boundless, eternal, supreme love, of whose greatness there is no end, yea, and His wisdom is infinite, whose peace passeth all understanding; since it is He who loves us, I say, can we think of repaying Him grudgingly? I will love Thee, O Lord, my strength. The Lord is my rock and my fortress and my deliverer, my God, my strength, in whom I will trust. He is all that I need, all that I long for.

Our limited love draws its meaning and depth from God's unlimited love.

Ps. 18:1 ff

My God and my help, I will love Thee for Thy great goodness; not so much as I might, surely, but as much as I can. I cannot love Thee as Thou deservest to be loved, for I cannot love Thee more than my own feebleness permits. I will love Thee more when Thou deemest me worthy to receive greater capacity for loving; yet never so perfectly as Thou hast deserved of me. Thine eyes did see my substance, yet being unperfect; and in Thy book all my members were written. Yet Thou recordest in that book all who do what

Our love grows by our willing acceptance of God's immeasureably greater love.

Ps. 139:16

But even when we definitely understand how our love draws on God's love, it still exceeds our understanding and our love. they can, even though they cannot do what they ought. Surely I have said enough to show how God should be loved and why.

But who has felt, who can know, who express, how much we should love him?

Pages 27 and 30: Edward Caswall's translation of a portion of St. Bernard's "Jesu, Dulcis Memoria."

JESU, THE VERY thought of thee With sweetness fills my breast; But sweeter far thy face to see, And in thy presence rest.

NOR VOICE CAN sing, nor heart can frame, Nor can the memory find, A sweeter sound than thy blest Name, O Saviour of mankind.

O JESU, THOU THE beauty art Of angel worlds above; Thy Name is music to the heart, Enchanting it with love.

Subit aīm dictare aliquid quod te op
timū Eugeni uł edificet uł delectet
uł consoletur. Sed nescio quo modo
uult & nō uult exire. leta quide sed lenta oro.
dum etenim illi contra imparate atendim ma
iestas aeq amor. Nempe urget ille inhibet illa.
sed intueueint dignatio tua qua hoc ipm nō ꝑcipis
sed petis. ni ꝑcipe magis te deceat. Maiestate tam
dignane cedente quid ni cedat pudor. Quid eni
si cathedram ascendisti. & si ambules sup penas
ventoru subderis in affectu. Amor dnium nescit
Agnoscit filiū & in filiis per se lacus subiectus e
Obsequiū sponte gratis obtemprat libere reuereretur
Non sic aliqui non sic sed aut timore ad ista impe
llitur aut cupiditate. Hi suc qui in facie bene
dicut mala aut in cordibus eorū. Hi blandiuntur
coram in netitate desiciunt. At caritas nuq excidit
Ego ut uerii fatear matris sum libatus officio sed
nec depdatus affectu. Olim mihi mulceras es
nō facile erueris. Ascende in celos descende in ab
yssos nō recedis a me sequar te quocuq ieris. Amini
paupem amabo paupu ac duntu patrem. Non sic
si bene te noui quia pr factus es pauperu ideo nō
pauper spu es. In te hanc mutacione factum esse
confido nō de te nec ꝑiri scitui tuo successisse, pmot
one sed accessisse. Monebo proinde te nō ut magi
sed ut mater. Plane uc amas amens magis uideur
sed ei qui nō amat ei qui uim nō senat amoris
Vnde iam ergo incipiam. Liber ab occupatiobs tuis
quia in his maxie condoleo tibi. Condoleo dixerim
si tu doles & tu. Alioqn doleo magis dixisse debuerā

O hOPE OF EVERY coฬtrite soul, **O** Joy of all the meek, how kind art thou to those who fall, how good to those who seek!

B UT WHΛT TO those who find? ah, this Nor tongue nor pen can shew: The love of Jesus, what it is, None but his lov'd ones know.

O JESU, SPOTLESS VIRGIN flower, Our life, our joy, to thee Be praise, beatitude, and power Through all eternity.

Chapter VII. How the hunger of man's heart cannot be satisfied with earthly things

ND NOW LET us consider what profit we shall have from loving God. Even though our knowledge of this is imperfect, still that is better than to ignore it altogether. I have already said (when it was a question of wherefore and in what manner God should be loved) that there was a double reason constraining us: His right and our advantage. Having written as best I can, though unworthily, of God's right to be loved. I have still to treat of the recompense which that love brings. For although God would be loved without respect of reward, yet He wills not to leave love unrewarded. True charity cannot be left destitute, even though she is unselfish and seeketh not her own. Love is an affection of the soul, not a contract: it cannot rise from a mere agreement, nor is it so to be gained. It is spontaneous in its origin and impulse; and true love is its own satisfaction. It has its reward; but that reward is the object beloved. For whatever you seem to love, if it is on account of something else, what you do really love is that something else, not the apparent object of desire. St. Paul did not preach the Gospel that he might earn his bread; he ate that he might be strengthened for his ministry. What he loved was not bread, but the Gospel. True love does not demand a reward, but it deserves one. Surely no one offers

God gives us the ability to love, and in His love gives us all other good things, too.

1 Cor. 13:5

Love is not utilitarian; trying to love God more, so as to get better rewards, will not work.

to pay for love; yet some recompense is due to one who loves, and if his love endures he will doubtless receive it.

On a lower plane of action, it is the reluctant, not the eager, whom we urge by promises of reward. Who would think of paying a man to do what he was yearning to do already? For instance no one would hire a hungry man to eat, or a thirsty man to drink, or a mother to nurse her own child. Who would think of bribing a farmer to dress his own vineyard, or to dig about his orchard, or to rebuild his house? So, all the more, one who loves God truly asks no other recompense than God Himself; for if he should demand anything else it would be the prize that he loved and not God.

Love leads from each natural good to greater goods; lesser goods cannot satisfy. It is natural for a man to desire what he reckons better than that which he has already, and be satisfied with nothing which lacks that special quality which he misses. Thus, if it is for her beauty that he loves his wife, he will cast longing eyes after a fairer woman. If he is clad in a rich garment, he will covet a costlier one; and no matter how rich he may be he will envy a man richer than himself. Do we not see people every day, endowed with vast estates, who keep on joining field to field, dreaming of wider boundaries for their lands?

Only a most lovely thing can make lesser things truly worth loving in themselves. Those who dwell in palaces are ever adding house to house, continually building up and tearing down, remodeling and changing. Men in high places are driven by insatiable ambition to clutch at still greater prizes. And nowhere is there any final satisfaction, because nothing there can be defined as absolutely the best or highest. But it is natural that nothing should content a man's desires but the very best, as he reckons it. Is it not, then, mad folly always to be craving for things which can never quiet our longings, much less satisfy them? No matter how many such things one has, he is always lusting after what he has not; never at peace, he sighs for new possessions. Discontented, he spends himself in fruitless toil, and finds only weariness in the evanescent and unreal pleasures of the world. In his greediness, he counts all that he has clutched as nothing in comparison with what is beyond his grasp, and loses all pleasure in his actual possessions by longing after what he has not, yet covets. No man can ever hope to own all things. Even the little one does possess is got only with toil and is held in fear; since each is certain to lose what he hath when God's day, appointed though unrevealed, shall come. But the perverted will struggles towards the ultimate good by devious ways, yearning after satisfaction, yet led astray by vanity and deceived by wickedness. Ah, if you wish to attain to the consummation of all desire, so that nothing unfulfilled will be left, why weary yourself with fruitless efforts, running hither and thither, only to die long before the goal is reached?

It is so that these impious ones wander in a circle, longing after something to gratify their yearnings, yet madly rejecting that which alone can bring them to their desired end, not by exhaustion but by attainment. They wear themselves out in vain travail, without reaching their blessed consummation, because they delight in creatures, not in the Creator. They

"Lust" is disordered desire; it means clinging to a lesser good at the expense of a greater, which sours and perverts that love.

Perverted loves either arise from or turn into rejections of greater goods, ultimately God.

want to traverse creation, trying all things one by one, rather than think of coming to Him who is Lord of all. And if their

Echoes St.
Augustine's
famous "our
hearts are
restless until
they find
their rest in
Thee."

utmost longing were realized, so that they should have all the world for their own, yet without possessing Him who is the Author of all being, then the same law of their desires would make them contemn what they had and restlessly seek Him whom they still lacked, that is, God Himself. Rest is in Him alone. Man knows no peace in the world; but he has no disturbance when he is with God. And so the soul says with confidence, Whom have I in heaven but Thee; and there is none upon earth that I desire in comparison of Thee.

Ps. 73:25 ff
Natural
knowledge
of God is
possible.

God is the strength of my heart, and my portion for ever. It is good for me to hold me fast by God, to put my trust in the Lord God. Even by this way one would eventually come to God, if only he might have time to test all lesser goods in turn.

Divine
revelation is
a practical
necessity for
mortals
with dis-
torted loves.

But life is too short, strength too feeble, and competitors too many, for that course to be practicable. One could never reach the end, though he were to weary himself with the long effort and fruitless toil of testing everything that might seem desirable. It would be far easier and better to make the

Reason pro-
portions our
loves.

assay in imagination rather than in experiment. For the mind is swifter in operation and keener in discrimination than the bodily senses, to this very purpose that it may go before the sensuous affections so that they may cleave to nothing which the mind has found worthless. And so it is written, Prove all

1 Thess. 5:21

things: hold fast that which is good. Which is to say that

right judgment should prepare the way for the heart. Otherwise we may not ascend into the hill of the Lord nor rise up in His holy place. We should have no profit in possessing a *Ps. 24:3* rational mind if we were to follow the impulse of the senses, like brute beasts, with no regard at all to reason. Those whom reason does not guide in their course may indeed run, but not in the appointed race-track, neglecting the apostolic counsel, So run that ye may obtain. For how could they *1 Cor. 9:24* obtain the prize who put that last of all in their endeavor and run round after everything else first?

But as for the righteous man, it is not so with him. He remembers the condemnation pronounced on the multitude who wander after vanity, who travel the broad way that leads to death; and he chooses the King's highway, turning *Matt. 7:13* aside neither to the right hand nor to the left, even as the *Num. 20:7* prophet saith, The way of the just is uprightness. Warned *Isa. 26:7* by wholesome counsel he shuns the perilous road, and heeds the direction that shortens the search, forbidding covetousness and commanding that he sell all that he hath and give *Matt. 19:21* to the poor. Blessed, truly, are the poor, for theirs is the Kingdom of Heaven. They which run in a race, run all, but *Matt. 5:3* distinction is made among the racers. The Lord knoweth the way of the righteous: and the way of the ungodly shall *Ps. 1:6* perish. A small thing that the righteous hath is better than great riches of the ungodly. Even as the Preacher saith, and *Ps. 37:16* the fool discovereth, He that loveth silver shall not be *Eccles. 5:10* satisfied with silver. But Christ saith, Blessed are they which do hunger and thirst after righteousness, for they shall be *Matt. 5:6* filled. Righteousness is the natural and essential food of the soul, which can no more be satisfied by earthly treasures than the hunger of the body can be satisfied by air. If you should see a starving man standing with mouth open to the wind, inhaling draughts of air as if in hope of gratifying his hunger, you would think him lunatic. But it is no less foolish to imagine that the soul can be satisfied with worldly things which only inflate it without feeding it. What have spiritual gifts to do with carnal appetites, or carnal with spiritual? Praise the Lord, O my soul: who satisfieth thy mouth with *Ps. 103:1 ff* good things. He bestows bounty immeasurable; He provokes thee to good, He preserves thee in goodness; He prevents, He sustains, He fills thee. He moves thee to longing, and it is He for whom thou longest.

Efficient causes lead from an initial state to a changed state. A final cause directs changes to an "object," or reason. I have said already that the motive for loving God is God Himself. And I spoke truly, for He is as well the efficient cause as the final object of our love. He gives the occasion for love, He creates the affection, He brings the desire to good effect. He is such that love to Him is a natural due; and so hope in Him is natural, since our present love would be vain did we not hope to love Him perfectly some day. Our love is prepared and rewarded by His. He loves us first, out of His great tenderness; then we are bound to repay Him with love; and we are permitted to cherish exultant hopes in *Rom. 10:12* Him. He is rich unto all that call upon Him, yet He has no gift for them better than Himself. He gives Himself as prize

and reward: He is the refreshment of holy soul, the ransom
of those in captivity. The Lord is good unto them that wait
for Him. What will He be then to those who gain His *Lam. 3:25*
presence? But here is a paradox, that no one can seek the
Lord who has not already found Him. It is Thy will, O God,
to be found that Thou mayest be sought, to be sought that
Thou mayest the more truly be found. But though Thou
canst be sought and found, Thou canst not be forestalled.
For if we say, Early shall my prayer come before Thee, yet *Ps. 88:13*
doubtless all prayer would be lukewarm unless it was ani-
mated by Thine inspiration.   *Ends come*
   We have spoken of the consummation of love towards *first; final*
God: now to consider whence such love begins.   *causes*
                                                                explain effi-
                                                                cient causes.

True
LOVE
does not
DEMAND
a reward,

but it
DESERVES
one.

Chapter VIII. The first degree of love: wherein man loves God for self's sake

L OVE IS ONE of the four natural affections, which it *"four natural* is needless to name since everyone knows them. And *affections":* because love is natural, it is only right to love the *love, fear, joy, sorrow.* Author of nature first of all. Hence comes the first and great commandment, Thou shalt love the Lord thy God. But *Matt. 22:37-* nature is so frail and weak that necessity compels her to love *38; Deut. 6:5* herself first; and this is carnal love, wherewith man loves himself first and selfishly, as it is written, That was not first which is spiritual but that which is natural; and afterward that which is spiritual. This is not as the precept ordains but *1 Cor. 15:46* as nature directs: No man ever yet hated his own flesh. But if, as is likely, this same love should grow excessive and, *Eph. 5:29* refusing to be contained within the restraining banks of necessity, should overflow into the fields of voluptuousness, then a command checks the flood, as if by a dike: Thou shalt *Matt. 22:39* love thy neighbor as thyself. And this is right: for he who shares our nature should share our love, itself the fruit of nature. Wherefore if a man find it a burden, I will not say only to relieve his brother's needs, but to minister to his brother's pleasures, let him mortify those same affections in himself, lest he become a transgressor. He may cherish himself as tenderly as he chooses, if only he remembers to show the same indulgence to his neighbor. This is the curb of temperance imposed on thee, O man, by the law of life

Personal sanctity & public morals go together. and conscience, lest thou shouldest follow thine own lusts to destruction, or become enslaved by those passions which are the enemies of thy true welfare. Far better divide thine enjoyments with thy neighbor than with these enemies. And if, after the counsel of the son of Sirach, thou goest not after *Ecclus. 18:30* thy desires but refrainest thyself from thine appetites; if according to the apostolic precept having food and raiment *1 Tim. 6:8* thou art therewith content, then thou wilt find it easy to abstain from fleshly lusts which war against the soul, and to divide with thy neighbors what thou hast refused to thine own desires. That is a temperate and righteous love which *Social love* practices self-denial in order to minister to a brother's *starts with* necessity. So our selfish love grows truly social, when it *hospitality.* includes our neighbors in its circle.

But if thou art reduced to want by such benevolence, what then? What indeed, except to pray with all confidence unto Him who giveth to all men liberally and upbraideth not, *James 1:5* who openeth His hand and filleth all things living with *Ps. 145:15* plenteousness. For doubtless He that giveth to most men more than they need will not fail thee as to the necessaries of life, even as He hath promised: Seek ye the Kingdom of *Luke 12:31* God, and all those things shall be added unto you. God freely promises all things needful to those who deny themselves for love of their neighbors; and to bear the yoke of modesty and sobriety, rather than to let sin reign in our *Rom. 6:12* mortal body, that is indeed to seek the Kingdom of God and to implore His aid against the tyranny of sin. It is surely justice to share our natural gifts with those who share our nature.

But if we are to love our neighbors as we ought, we must *Each per-* have regard to God also: for it is only in God that we can pay *son's love,* that debt of love aright. Now a man cannot love his neighbor *and each other's loveli-* in God, except he love God Himself; wherefore we must love *ness, both* God first, in order to love our neighbors in Him. This too, *begin and* like all good things, is the Lord's doing, that we should love *end in* Him, for He hath endowed us with the possibility of love. *God's love;* He who created nature sustains it; nature is so constituted *the order is important.* that its Maker is its protector for ever. Without Him nature could not have begun to be; without Him it could not subsist at all. That we might not be ignorant of this, or *Suffering* vainly attribute to ourselves the beneficence of our Creator, *can help us* God has determined in the depths of His wise counsel that *realize our* we should be subject to tribulations. So when man's strength *neediness and put our* fails and God comes to his aid, it is meet and right that man, *loves back in* rescued by God's hand, should glorify Him, as it is written, *order.* Call upon Me in the time of trouble; so will I hear thee, and thou shalt praise Me' (Ps. 50.15). In such wise man, animal *Ps. 50:15* and carnal by nature, and loving only himself, begins to love God by reason of that very self-love; since he learns that in God he can accomplish all things that are good, and that *John 15:5* without God he can do nothing.

Our selfish
LOVE
grows truly
SOCIAL,
when it includes our
NEIGHBORS
in its
CIRCLE.

Chapter IX. The second and third degrees of love

SO THEN IN the beginning man loves God, not for God's sake, but for his own. It is something for him to know how little he can do by himself and how much by God's help, and in that knowledge to order himself rightly towards God, his sure support. But when tribulations, recurring again and again, constrain him to turn to God for unfailing help, would not even a heart as hard as iron, as cold as marble, be softened by the goodness of such a Savior, so that he would love God not altogether selfishly, but because He is God? Let frequent troubles drive us to frequent supplications; and surely, tasting, we must see how gracious the Lord is (Ps. 34.8). Thereupon His goodness once realized draws us to love Him unselfishly, yet more than our own needs impel us to love Him selfishly: even as the Samaritans told the woman who announced that it was Christ who was at the well: Now we believe, not because of thy saying: for we have heard Him ourselves, and know that this is indeed the Christ, the savior of the world. We likewise bear the same witness to our own fleshly nature, saying, No longer do we love God because of our necessity, but because we have tasted and seen how gracious the Lord is'. Our temporal wants have a speech of their own, proclaiming the benefits they have received from God's favor. Once this is recognized it will not be hard to fulfill the commandment touching love to our neighbors; for whosoever loves God

Dependency, "like a little child," leads us into deeper experiences of God's love.

Returning God's love, even the tiniest bit, leads us deeper.

Ps. 34:8

John 4:42

Whoever loves God, loves what He loves.

1 Peter 1:22

1 John 3:18

aright loves all God's creatures. Such love is pure, and finds no burden in the precept bidding us purify our souls, in obeying the truth through the Spirit unto unfeigned love of the brethren. Loving as he ought, he counts that command only just. Such love is thankworthy, since it is spontaneous; pure, since it is shown not in word nor tongue, but in deed and truth; just, since it repays what it has received. Whoso loves in this fashion, loves even as he is loved, and seeks no more his own but the things which are Christ's, even as Jesus sought not His own welfare, but ours, or rather ourselves.

Ps. 118:1

Such was the psalmist's love when he sang: O give thanks unto the Lord, for He is gracious. Whosoever praises God for His essential goodness, and not merely because of the benefits He has bestowed, does really love God for God's sake, and not selfishly. The psalmist was not speaking of such

Ps. 49:18

love when he said: So long as thou doest well unto thyself, men will speak good of thee. The third degree of love, we have now seen, is to love God on His own account, solely because He is God.

Chapter X. The fourth degree of love: wherein man does not even love self except for God's sake

OW BLESSED IS he who reaches the fourth degree of love, wherein one loves himself only in God! Thy righteousness standeth like the strong mountains, O God. Such love as this is God's hill, in the which it pleaseth Him to dwell. Who shall ascend into the hill of the Lord? O *Ps. 24:3* that I had wings like a dove; for then would I flee away and *Ps. 55:6* be at rest. At Salem is His tabernacle; and His dwelling in *Ps. 76:2* Sion. Woe is me, that I am constrained to dwell with Mesech! *Ps. 120:5* When shall this flesh and blood, this earthen vessel which is my soul's tabernacle, attain thereto? When shall my soul, *God's love* rapt with divine love and altogether self-forgetting, yea, *is completely* become like a broken vessel, yearn wholly for God, and, *the cause* *of ours.* joined unto the Lord, be one spirit with Him? When shall she exclaim, My flesh and my heart faileth; but God is the *Ps. 73:26* strength of my heart and my portion for ever. I would count him blessed and holy to whom such rapture has been *So even* vouchsafed in this mortal life, for even an instant to lose *slight direct* thyself, as if thou wert emptied and lost and swallowed up *experience* in God, is no human love; it is celestial. But if sometimes a *of loving* poor mortal feels that heavenly joy for a rapturous moment, *like God,* then this wretched life envies his happiness, the malice of *or truly* daily trifles disturbs him, this body of death weighs him *loving God,* down, the needs of the flesh are imperative, the weakness of *our usual* corruption fails him, and above all brotherly love calls him *sense of self.*

back to duty. Alas! that voice summons him to re-enter his own round of existence; and he must ever cry out lamentably, *Isa. 38:14* O Lord, I am oppressed: undertake for me; and again, O wretched man that I am! who shall deliver me from the body *Rom. 7:24* of this death?

Seeing that the Scripture saith, God has made all for His *Isa. 43:7* own glory, surely His creatures ought to conform themselves, as much as they can, to His will. In Him should all our affections center, so that in all things we should seek only to do His will, not to please ourselves. And real happiness will come, not in gratifying our desires or in gaining transient pleasures, but in accomplishing God's will for us: even as we *Matt. 6:10* pray every day: Thy will be done in earth as it is in heaven. O chaste and holy love! O sweet and gracious affection! O *Even the* pure and cleansed purpose, thoroughly washed and purged *suffering of* from any admixture of selfishness, and sweetened by contact *returning to* with the divine will! To reach this state is to become godlike. *everyday-* *ness and* As a drop of water poured into wine loses itself, and takes *distraction* the color and savor of wine; or as a bar of iron, heated *thus* red-hot, becomes like fire itself, forgetting its own nature; *becomes an* or as the air, radiant with sun-beams, seems not so much to *occasion for* *deeper love* be illuminated as to be light itself; so in the saints all human *of God.* affections melt away by some unspeakable transmutation into the will of God. For how could God be all in all, if *Not merely* anything merely human remained in man? The substance *human, but* will endure, but in another beauty, a higher power, a greater *gloriously* glory. When will that be? Who will see, who possess it? *human.*

When shall I come to appear before the presence of God? *Ps. 42:2*
My heart hath talked of Thee, Seek ye My face: Thy face,
Lord, will I seek. Lord, thinkest Thou that I, even I shall see *Ps. 27:8*
Thy holy temple?

In this life, I think, we cannot fully and perfectly obey that
precept, Thou shalt love the Lord thy God with all thy heart,
and with all thy soul, and with all thy strength, and with all
thy mind. For here the heart must take thought for the body; *Luke 10:27*
and the soul must energize the flesh; and the strength must
guard itself from impairment. And by God's favor, must *St. Bernard*
seek to increase. It is therefore impossible to offer up all our *suffered*
being to God, to yearn altogether for His face, so long as we *from serious*
health prob-
must accommodate our purposes and aspirations to these *lems, and*
fragile, sickly bodies of ours. Wherefore the soul may hope *was fre-*
to possess the fourth degree of love, or rather to be possessed *quently sum-*
by it, only when it has been clothed upon with that spiritual *moned from*
his prayers
and immortal body, which will be perfect, peaceful, lovely, *to meet the*
and in everything wholly subjected to the spirit. And to this *needs of*
degree no human effort can attain: it is in God's power to *the day.*
give it to whom He wills. Then the soul will easily reach that *This conflict*
is his experi-
highest stage, because no lusts of the flesh will retard its eager *ence as*
entrance into the joy of its Lord, and no troubles will disturb *much as*
its peace. May we not think that the holy martyrs enjoyed *ours.*
this grace, in some degree at least, before they laid down their
victorious bodies? Surely that was immeasurable strength
of love which enraptured their souls, enabling them to laugh
at fleshly torments and to yield their lives gladly. But even

Sounds wry, but reminds us that we humans always love God in our bodies. though the frightful pain could not destroy their peace of mind, it must have impaired somewhat its perfection.

Chapter XI. The perfect love attained at the resurrection

WHAT OF THE souls already released from their bodies? We believe that they are overwhelmed in that vast sea of eternal light and of luminous eternity. But no one denies that they still hope and desire to receive their bodies again: whence it is plain that they are not yet wholly transformed, and that something of self remains yet unsurrendered. Not until death is swallowed up in victory, and perennial light overflows the uttermost bounds of darkness, not until celestial glory clothes our bodies, can our souls be freed entirely from self and give themselves up to God. For until then souls are bound to bodies, if not by a vital connection of sense, still by natural affection; so that without their bodies they cannot attain to their perfect consummation, nor would they if they could. And although there is no defect in the soul itself before the restoration of its body, since it has already attained to the highest state of which it is by itself capable, yet the spirit would not yearn for reunion with the flesh if without the flesh it could be consummated.

And finally, Right dear in the sight of the Lord is the death of His saints. But if their death is precious, what must such a life as theirs be! No wonder that the body shall seem to add fresh glory to the spirit; for though it is weak and mortal, it has availed not a little for mutual help. How truly he spake who said, All things work together for good to them that

A difficult passage! That union with God remains partial until Resurrection fits, but why "unsurrendered"? Bernard believes firmly that body & soul act together, so if God has not yet reunited body and soul, He is still drawing the soul into His perfect love. Ps. 116.15

Rom. 8:28 love God. The body is a help to the soul that loves God, even when it is ill, even when it is dead, and all the more when it is raised again from the dead: for illness is an aid to penitence; death is the gate of rest; and the resurrection will bring *"Would"* consummation. So, rightly, the soul would not be perfected *means "does* without the body, since she recognizes that in every condi- *not wish to," * *here.* tion it has been needful to her good.

The flesh then is a good and faithful comrade for a good soul: since even when it is a burden it assists; when the help ceases, the burden ceases too; and when once more the assistance begins, there is no longer a burden. The first state is toilsome, but fruitful; the second is idle, but not monotonous: the third is glorious. Hear how the Bridegroom in *Cant. 5:1* Canticles bids us to this threefold progress: Eat, O friends; drink, yea, drink abundantly, O beloved' (Cant. 5.1). He *Spiritual* offers food to those who are laboring with bodily toil; then *reading of* He calls the resting souls whose bodies are laid aside, to *Song of* drink; and finally He urges those who have resumed their *Solomon* bodies to drink abundantly. Surely those He styles beloved' *here used* must overflow with charity; and that is the difference *to describe,* between them and the others, whom He calls not beloved' *from* *another* but friends'. Those who yet groan in the body are dear to *angle, how* Him, according to the love that they have; those released *grace heals* from the bonds of flesh are dearer because they have become *and perfects* *nature.* readier and abler to love than hitherto. But beyond either of these classes are those whom He calls beloved': for they have received the second garment, that is, their glorified bodies, so that now nothing of self remains to hinder or disturb them, and they yield themselves eagerly and entirely to loving God. This cannot be so with the others; for the first have the weight of the body to bear, and the second desires the body again with something of selfish expectation.

At first then the faithful soul eats her bread, but alas! in the sweat of her face. Dwelling in the flesh, she walks as yet by faith, which must work through love. As faith without works is dead, so work itself is food for her; even as our Lord saith, My meat is to do the will of Him that sent Me. When *John 4:34* the flesh is laid aside, she eats no more the bread of carefulness, but is allowed to drink deeply of the wine of love, as if after a repast.

But the wine is not yet unmingled; even as the Bridegroom saith in another place, I have drunk My wine with My milk' (Cant. 5.1). For the soul mixes with the wine of God's love *Cant. 5:1* the milk of natural affection, that is, the desire for her body *This image* and its glorification. She glows with the wine of holy love *of growing* which she has drunk; but she is not yet all on fire, for she has *taste, toler-* tempered the potency of that wine with milk. The unmin- *ance, and* *appetite* gled wine would enrapture the soul and make her wholly *for bread* unconscious of self; but here is no such transport for she is *and wine* still desirous of her body. When that desire is appeased, when *may help* *many of us* the one lack is supplied, what should hinder her then from *who find* yielding herself utterly to God, losing her own likeness and *this chapter* being made like unto Him? At last she attains to that chalice *hard going.* of the heavenly wisdom, of which it is written, My cup shall be full. Now indeed she is refreshed with the abundance of the house of God, where all selfish, carking care is done away, and where, for ever safe, she drinks the fruit of the vine, new *Matt. 26:29* and pure, with Christ in the Kingdom of His Father.

It is Wisdom who spreads this threefold supper where all the repast is love; Wisdom who feeds the toilers, who gives drink to those who rest, who floods with rapture those that reign with Christ. Even as at an earthly banquet custom and nature serve meat first and then wine, so here. Before death, while we are still in mortal flesh, we eat the labors of our hands, we swallow with an effort the food so gained; but after death, we shall begin eagerly to drink in the spiritual life and finally, reunited to our bodies, and rejoicing in fullness of delight, we shall be refreshed with immortality. This is what the Bridegroom means when He saith: Eat, O *Cant. 5:1* friends; drink, yea, drink abundantly, O beloved.' Eat before death; begin to drink after death; drink abundantly after the resurrection. Rightly are they called beloved who have drunk abundantly of love; rightly do they drink abundantly who *Rev. 19:9* are worthy to be brought to the marriage supper of the *Luke 22:30* Lamb, eating and drinking at His table in His Kingdom. At that supper, He shall present to Himself a glorious Church, *Eph. 5:27* not having spot, or wrinkle, or any such thing. Then truly shall He refresh His beloved; then He shall give them drink *Ps. 36:8* of His pleasures, as out of the river. While the Bridegroom clasps the Bride in tender, pure embrace, then the rivers of *Ps. 46:4* the flood thereof shall make glad the city of God. And this refers to the Son of God Himself, who will come forth and serve them, even as He hath promised; so that in that day the righteous shall be glad and rejoice before God: they shall also be merry and joyful. Here indeed is appeasement *Ps. 68:3* without weariness: here never-quenched thirst for knowledge, without distress; here eternal and infinite desire which knows no want; here, finally, is that sober inebriation which comes not from drinking new wine but from enjoying God. *Acts 2:13* The fourth degree of love is attained for ever when we love God only and supremely, when we do not even love our- *Here, St.* selves except for God's sake; so that He Himself is the reward *Bernard* of them that love Him, the everlasting reward of an everlast- *reaches the* *conclusion* ing love. *of his main* *exposition.*

What follows in Chapters XII-XV is an excerpt from a similar long letter written to the Carthusian monks. Although St. Bernard was an influential early Cistercian, he maintained lively interactions with the Carthusians and Victorines, among many others.

RIGHTLY

are they called

BELOVED

who have drunk

ABUNDANTLY

of
LOVE

Chapter XII. From a letter to the Carthusians

I REMEMBER WRITING A letter to the holy Carthusian brethren, wherein I discussed these degrees of love, and spoke of charity in other words, although not in another sense, than here. It may be well to repeat a portion of that letter, since it is easier to copy than to dictate anew.

Bernard's Cistercians started at Citeaux; Carthusians in the Chartreuse Valley.

To love our neighbor's welfare as much as our own: that is true and sincere charity out of a pure heart, and of a good conscience, and of faith unfeigned. Whosoever loves his own prosperity only is proved thereby not to love good for its own sake, since he loves it on his own account. And so he cannot sing with the psalmist, O give thanks unto the Lord, for He is gracious. Such a man would praise God, not because He is goodness, but because He has been good to him: he could take to himself the reproach of the same writer, So long as Thou doest well unto him, he will speak good of Thee. One praises God because He is mighty, another because He is gracious, yet another solely because He is essential goodness. The first is a slave and fears for himself; the second is greedy, desiring further benefits; but the third is a son who honors his Father. He who fears, he who profits, are both concerned about self-interest. Only in the son is that charity which seeketh not her own. Wherefore I take this saying, The law of the Lord is an undefiled law, converting the soul to be of charity; because charity alone is able to turn the soul away from love of self and of the world to pure

1 Tim. 1:5

Ps. 118.1

Ps. 49:18, Vulg.

1 Cor. 13:5

Ps. 19:7

love of God. Neither fear nor self-interest can convert the *Reforming* soul. They may change the appearance, perhaps even the *behavior is* conduct, but never the object of supreme desire. Sometimes *not, in itself,* a slave may do God's work; but because he does not toil *conversion.* voluntarily, he remains in bondage. So a mercenary may serve God, but because he puts a price on his service, he is enchained by his own greediness. For where there is self-interest there is isolation; and such isolation is like the dark corner of a room where dust and rust befoul. Fear is the motive which constrains the slave; greed binds the selfish *James 1:14* man, by which he is tempted when he is drawn away by his own lust and enticed. But neither fear nor self-interest is undefiled, nor can they convert the soul. Only charity can convert the soul, freeing it from unworthy motives.

Next, I call it undefiled because it never keeps back anything of its own for itself. When a man boasts of nothing as his very own, surely all that he has is God's; and what is God's cannot be unclean. The undefiled law of the Lord is that love which bids men seek not their own, but every man another's wealth. It is called the law of the Lord as much because He lives in accordance with it as because no man has it except by gift from Him. Nor is it improper to say that even God lives by law, when that law is the law of love. For what preserves the glorious and ineffable Unity of the blessed Trinity, except love? Charity, the law of the Lord, joins the Three Persons into the unity of the Godhead and unites the holy Trinity in the bond of peace. Do not suppose me to imply that charity exists as an accidental quality of Deity; for whatever could be conceived of as wanting in the divine Nature is not God. No, it is the very substance of the Godhead; and my assertion is neither novel nor extraordinary, since St. John says, 'God is love' (I John 4.8). One may *1 John 4:8* therefore say with truth that love is at once God and the gift of God, essential love imparting the quality of love. Where *Human* the word refers to the Giver, it is the name of His very being; *love is* where the gift is meant, it is the name of a quality. Love is *ruled by* the eternal law whereby the universe was created and is ruled. *the forces* Since all things are ordered in measure and number and *of nature,* weight, and nothing is left outside the realm of law, that *but God's* universal law cannot itself be without a law, which is itself. *love is* So love though it did not create itself, does surely govern *what gives* itself by its own decree. *nature its laws.*

LOVE
is the eternal
LAW
whereby the universe
WAS CREATED
and
IS RULED

Chapter XIII. The law of self-will and desire

FURTHERMORE, THE SLAVE and the hireling have a law, not from the Lord, but of their own contriving; the one does not love God, the other loves something else more than God. They have a law of their own, not of God, I say; yet it is subject to the law of the Lord. For though they can make laws for themselves, they cannot supplant the changeless order of the eternal law. Each man is a law unto himself, when he sets up his will against the universal law, perversely striving to rival his Creator, to be wholly independent, making his will his only law. What a heavy and burdensome yoke upon all the sons of Adam, bowing down our necks, so that our life draweth nigh unto hell. O wretched man that I am! Who shall deliver me from the body of this death? I am weighed down, I am almost overwhelmed, so that If the Lord had not helped me, it had not failed but my soul had been put to silence. Job was groaning under this load when he lamented: Why hast Thou set me as a mark against Thee, so that I am a burden to myself? He was a burden to himself through the law which was of his own devising: yet he could not escape God's law, for he was set as a mark against God. The eternal law of righteousness ordains that he who will not submit to God's sweet rule shall suffer the bitter tyranny of self: but he who wears the easy yoke and light burden of love will escape the intolerable weight of his own self-will. Wondrously and

Even false loves start from goods and are intended to be ordered to love of God.

Rom. 7:24

Ps. 94:17

Job 7:20

Matt. 11:30

justly does that eternal law retain rebels in subjection, so that
Ignoring they are unable to escape. They are subject to God's power,
natural law yet deprived of happiness with Him, unable to dwell with
does not God in light and rest and glory everlasting. O Lord my God,
nullify it.
Job 7:21 why dost Thou not pardon my transgression and take away
mine iniquity? Then freed from the weight of my own will,
I can breathe easily under the light burden of love. I shall
not be coerced by fear, nor allured by mercenary desires; for
I shall be led by the Spirit of God, that free Spirit whereby
Rom. 8:16 Thy sons are led, which beareth witness with my spirit that
I am among the children of God. So shall I be under that
law which is Thine; and as Thou art, so shall I be in the world.
Rom. 13:8 Whosoever do what the apostle bids, Owe no man anything,
but to love one another, are doubtless even in this life
conformed to God's likeness: they are neither slaves nor
hirelings but sons.

Chapter XIV. The law of the love of sons

NOW THE CHILDREN have their law, even though it is written, The law is not made for a righteous man. For it must be remembered that *1 Tim. 1:9* there is one law having to do with the spirit of servitude, given to fear, and another with the spirit of liberty, given in tenderness. The children are not constrained by the first, yet they could not exist without the second: even as St. Paul writes, Ye have not received the spirit of bondage again to fear; but ye have received the spirit of adoption, whereby we cry, Abba, Father. And again to show that that same righ- *Rom. 8:15* teous man was not under the law, he says: To them that are under the law, I became as under the law, that I might gain them that are under the law; to them that are without law, as without law (being not without law to God, but under the law to Christ). So it is rightly said, not that the righteous *1 Cor. 9:20 ff* do not have a law, but, The law is not made for a righteous man', that is, it is not imposed on rebels but freely given to those willingly obedient, by Him whose goodness estab- lished it. Wherefore the Lord saith meekly: Take My yoke *Matt. 11:29* upon you, which may be paraphrased thus: I do not force it on you, if you are reluctant; but if you will you may bear it. Otherwise it will be weariness, not rest, that you shall find for your souls.

Love is a good and pleasant law; it is not only easy to bear, but it makes the laws of slaves and hirelings tolerable; not destroying but completing them; as the Lord saith: I am not

Matt. 5:17 come to destroy the law, but to fulfill. It tempers the fear of the slave, it regulates the desires of the hireling, it mitigates

Throughout this work, things like fear, desire, body, love, can exist in godly or perverse form. the severity of each. Love is never without fear, but it is godly fear. Love is never without desire, but it is lawful desire. So love perfects the law of service by infusing devotion; it perfects the law of wages by restraining covetousness. Devotion mixed with fear does not destroy it, but purges it. Then the burden of fear which was intolerable while it was only servile, becomes tolerable; and the fear itself remains ever

1 John 4:18 pure and filial. For though we read: Perfect love casteth out fear' (I John 4.18), we understand by that the suffering which

Self-interest can be just within limits. is never absent from servile fear, the cause being put for the effect, as often elsewhere. So, too, self-interest is restrained within due bounds when love supervenes; for then it rejects evil things altogether, prefers better things to those merely

God's grace converts each of these rela- tions into a still better ordered form. good, and cares for the good only on account of the better. In like manner, by God's grace, it will come about that man will love his body and all things pertaining to his body, for the sake of his soul. He will love his soul for God's sake; and he will love God for Himself alone.

Chapter XV. The four degrees of love

NEVERTHELESS, SINCE WE are carnal and are born of the lust of the flesh, it must be that our desire and our love shall have its beginning in the flesh. But rightly guided by the grace of God through these degrees, it will have its consummation in the spirit: for that was not first which is spiritual but that which is natural; and afterward that which is spiritual. And we must bear the image of the earthy first, before we can bear the image of the heavenly. At first, man loves himself for his own sake. That is the flesh, which can appreciate nothing beyond itself. Next, he perceives that he cannot exist by himself, and so begins by faith to seek after God, and to love Him as something necessary to his own welfare. That is the second degree, to love God, not for God's sake, but selfishly. But when he has learned to worship God and to seek Him aright, meditating on God, reading God's Word, praying and obeying His commandments, he comes gradually to know what God is, and finds Him altogether lovely. So, having tasted and seen how gracious the Lord is (Ps. 34.8), he advances to the third degree, when he loves God, not merely as his benefactor but as God. Surely he must remain long in this state; and I know not whether it would be possible to make further progress in this life to that fourth degree and perfect condition wherein man loves himself solely for God's sake. Let any who have attained so far bear record; I confess it seems beyond

Note this is not spirit versus body, but natural body & spiritual body.

1 Cor. 15:46

Ps. 34:8

Humility and self-knowledge, here.

my powers. Doubtless it will be reached when the good and
Matt. 25:21 faithful servant shall have entered into the joy of his Lord,
Ps. 36:8 and been satisfied with the plenteousness of God's house.
For then in wondrous wise he will forget himself and as if
delivered from self, he will grow wholly God's. Joined unto
1 Cor. 6:17 the Lord, he will then be one spirit with Him. This was what
the prophet meant, I think, when he said: I will go forth in
the strength of the Lord God: and will make mention of Thy
Ps. 71:16 righteousness only. Surely he knew that when he should go
forth in the spiritual strength of the Lord, he would have
been freed from the infirmities of the flesh, and would have
nothing carnal to think of, but would be wholly filled in his
spirit with the righteousness of the Lord.

In that day the members of Christ can say of themselves
what St. Paul testified concerning their Head: Yea, though
we have known Christ after the flesh, yet now henceforth
2 Cor. 5:16 know we Him no more. None shall thereafter know himself
after the flesh; for flesh and blood cannot inherit the
1 Cor. 15:50 Kingdom of God. Not that there will be no true substance
A spiritual of the flesh, but all carnal needs will be taken away, and the
body is a love of the flesh will be swallowed up in the love of the spirit,
phsyical so that our weak human affections will be made divinely
body per-
fectly strong. Then the net of charity which as it is drawn through
ordered. the great and wide sea doth not cease to gather every kind of
Matt. 13:48 fish, will be drawn to the shore; and the bad will be cast away,
while only the good will be kept. In this life the net of
all-including love gathers every kind of fish into its wide folds,

becoming all things to all men, sharing adversity or prosperity, rejoicing with them that do rejoice, and weeping with them that weep. But when the net is drawn to shore, *Rom. 12:15* whatever causes pain will be rejected, like the bad fish, while only what is pleasant and joyous will be kept. Do you not recall how St. Paul said: Who is weak and I am not weak? *2 Cor. 11:29* Who is offended and I burn not?' And yet weakness and offense were far from him. So too he bewailed many which had sinned already and had not repented, though he was neither the sinner nor the penitent. But there is a city made glad by the rivers of the flood of grace, and whose gates the *Ps. 46:4* Lord loveth more than all the dwellings of Jacob. In it is no *Ps. 87:2* place for lamentation over those condemned to everlasting fire, prepared for the devil and his angels. In these earthly *Matt 25:41* dwellings, though men may rejoice, yet they have still other battles to fight, other mortal perils to undergo. But in the heavenly Fatherland no sorrow nor sadness can enter: as it *Ps. 87:7,* is written, The habitation of all rejoicing ones is in Thee; *Vulg.* and again, Everlasting joy shall be unto them. Nor could they *Isa. 61:7* recall things piteous, for then they will make mention of God's righteousness only. Accordingly, there will be no need for the exercise of compassion, for no misery will be there to inspire pity.

Printed in the USA
CPSIA information can be obtained
at www.ICGtesting.com
LVHW070952111123
763674LV00001B/8